AF530842

Also by Gayle Graham:

How to Home School, A Practical Approach

How to Teach Any Child to SPELL

by Gayle Graham, M.Ed.

Common Sense Press
8786 Highway 21
P.O. Box 1365
Melrose, FL 32666
(904) 475-5757

Printed in the United States of America.

ISBN 1-880892-23-5

Dedicated to Heather and Amy,
who both learned
how to spell.

Table of Contents

Introduction

Amy learned to read later than most children. Even though I diligently followed at least three different reading curricula in succession (all guaranteed by my homeschooling friends) over a period of four years, Amy did not read fluently until age ten.

Spelling followed even more slowly. Amy's a thoughtful child, and thoughtful people have important things to say to the rest of us. But how can they communicate in writing if they can't spell? Sure, Amy dutifully memorized massive word lists. She memorized phonics flashcards and completed countless spelling worksheets. But when she composed a simple paragraph, Amy spelled a common word like **'went'**: **'whent'**.

When she was twelve-years-old Amy's standardized tests confirmed our deepest concerns. Her spelling scores fell below the 20th percentile! Now, you'd think I'd know what to do about the problem. After all, my master's degree was in learning disabilities and I wrote my graduate study on, (what else), "Teaching Spelling." But none of the theory I'd learned worked!

I read Ruth Beechick's comparison of spelling approaches in *You Can Teach Your Child Successfully.* Since I'd already tried the common word list and the workbook approach, I decided to try the individualized method. Dr. Beechick suggests with this method that parents teach the children words they miss in their own writing. It makes sense. Learn to spell the specific words that give you the most trouble. But for Amy, memorizing individualized spelling lists wasn't enough. She needed something more to sink her teeth into.

Sometimes the best ideas are the simplest. I decided to take Ruth Beechick's suggestion one step further. Why not create a simple individualized spelling notebook? Put one spelling (not reading) rule on each page. Help Amy categorize her own spelling mistakes under the proper rule. Discuss the reason for each error when it arises and develop a strategy together for remembering the word's spelling. Drill Amy's own misspelled words daily for 3-5 minutes. Amy agreed to cooperate with me on this experiment. After all, she was as desperate as I was. For one whole year she and I carefully analyzed her spelling mistakes (from her own writing) and categorized them. We discovered her errors all clustered under a few rules. For example, to this day, Amy knows to listen carefully to words of three or more syllables that have a short 'e' sound. Is that a short 'e' or a short 'i' I'm hearing? (We Virginians are always mixing up our 'e' and 'i' sounds. Benefit becomes benifit, hemline becomes himline.)

The result? In one year, Amy's spelling scores rose 20 percentile points. The next year they rose another 20 percentile points. Today, (three years later), Amy's spelling is superior. If she doesn't know how to spell a word, she *notices* it and corrects the word with a dictionary. Isn't that what we're after?

Generally speaking, poor spellers have one thing in common. They don't remember how a word should look. If they did, they would self-correct when they proofread their papers. This past school year I asked my high school humanities class (all homeschoolers) how many of them would like to solve their spelling problems? How would they like it if they could stop misspelling words in their papers? Two-thirds of the children instantly raised their hands. I warned them the approach might seem a little simple for high schoolers but I encouraged them to ask fifteen-year-old Amy if it worked.

A broad grin spread across Amy's face. "Believe me. It works!" she exclaimed.

"We'll do anything you say, Mrs. Graham, if we can learn how to spell."

I saw an immediate improvement in the spelling of the young people who used (and reviewed) their spelling notebooks. Poor spellers who overcome their problem have something in common. They pinpoint their own areas of need and then learn to pay careful attention to detail when they proofread their own writing. Since our language is so predictable, it's really not that hard to do IF we have the right tools.

This individualized spelling notebook that accompanies this manual is a tool. I believe with all my heart that anyone who uses it can overcome his or her spelling problems. Poor spellers avoid writing. I want your children to write freely without inhibition! How else will they be able to communicate their thoughts to a needy world?

P. S. to Moms and Teachers:

Not all children need the approach described in this manual in order to learn to spell. If your child is picking up spelling naturally in the context of reading and writing, he needs neither this book nor other spelling workbooks. Lead him into other areas of study.

Foreword

Most letter combinations in our language are highly predictable. For example, the combination **'ai'** has the long **a** sound as in **rain** 98% of the time. Two exceptions are **aisle** (where **ai** says the long i sound) and **said** where **ai** has the short **e** sound). Common sense tells me it is a waste of time to teach a rule for **'ai'** in **aisle** or **said**. Instead, we treat these words as exceptions to be learned. Most children can handle that a lot better than "rule overload."

Most older children have a reasonable grasp of the sounds of individual consonants and consonant blends. Therefore, I've not included pages in the student's notebook, ***Tricks of the Trade*** for those sounds. They usually can hear and write short vowels correctly in one syllable words, but often break down in words of three or more syllables. Simply categorize the word according to the syllable that had the problem. For example, if a child spelled **competent**, **compitent**, that word would be written on the 'short **e**' page in the student's notebook.

❦ Chapter 1 ❦

Spelling Myths

Let's start our discussion on teaching spelling by dispelling a few myths. Deep down inside you may have known all along these were myths, but if you're like me, you were afraid to trust your gut instincts.

The first myth is, **"Good spellers memorize lots of spelling rules."**

Maybe you learned to spell like I did. You learned to read and you read widely. You tried to write. After lots of reading practice, you began to notice when a word you wrote "looked funny." If a word "looked funny" you tried it another way. Why do some people spell well? Because they have good visual memories. Visual memory is the key to good spelling. So, if you happen to be a person with a strong visual memory, you remember how words look. You write a word and take a look at it. You say, "That looks funny. Let me try it a different way." Then you change a letter or two and say, "Now that looks right." That's exactly how a person learns to spell! Memorizing rules before you even <u>try</u> to spell is not the best way to learn to spell.

The second myth is **"Doing lots of spelling worksheets makes good spellers."** Spelling is really complex thinking which occurs *as you're writing.* We can't learn to spell from workbooks alone. We learn principles about the way words are formed—the system of our language—with spelling workbooks. That's great! But a poor speller won't learn to be a good speller from workbooks. A poor speller will learn to spell from *writing*, followed by an *analysis* of his own errors, followed by *drill* and more *practice*.

Writing gives your speller the chance to try out spelling patterns and words. It gives him the opportunity to think for himself, "Oh, I've seen it this way." Besides the visual recollection of how the word should look, there has to be some time for reflection. What do I recall? What have I learned about how to spell the sound **/ow/**? When a child practices spelling in the context of writing, he learns to spell! He won't learn to spell by being told, "Fill in the blanks from the list." He'll learn to spell from being required to use and analyze what he's learned in the context of his own writing.

Some of you have good spellers at your house. You don't know how they learned to spell. But they learned to read, and a year or two later they were spelling. So how did your good spellers learn to spell? They became good spellers because of their strong visual memories coupled with their ability to sequence sounds (hear syllables.)

Poor spellers don't recall the way a word should look. Let's give them the opportunity to think about it. Instead of spending a lot of time in workbooks, practice **free writing** followed by **categorizing the child's own misspelled words** (according to the syllable patterns of our language) in an individualized spelling notebook. The student experiments with spelling in his own writing. Then we gently guide him in categorizing his own misspellings in a notebook. Rules are applied only as needed. Sure seems a lot easier to me!

Myth number three: **"Memorizing lists of words for a spelling test will make my child a good speller."** What about the child who makes straight A's on the spelling test and then misspells the very same words next week in his own writing? Memorization is not enough to solve the problem for poor spellers.

The most destructive myth: **"Good teachers always correct <u>every</u> misspelled word."** Go right ahead if your goal is to create 'writer's block'! Ever have a child who can't think of anything to write? Think back. What do you do to the papers he *does* write?!

A secure child (one not subject to ridicule or a 'put-down') is willing to take risks—to try something challenging. The other night at dinner, six-year-old Meg wrote on her napkin, "I can ride my <u>bick</u>." (Translate that: 'bike'.) I marveled at her application of the most recent phonics rule we had learned in reading: "ck" says /k/ at the end of a word. There was no way I was about to correct her—yet. She'll figure out her own error as she becomes a more fluent reader. Save absolute accountability for "published" pieces—like the letter they're sending to grandma (especially if grandma happens to be skeptical about homeschooling!) The choice is yours: Use the "Open up" or "Clam up" approach.

And the silliest myth of all: **Writing a misspelled word 10 times will help you learn it.** Oh yeah? Try it and see.

❦ Chapter 2 ❦

Stages & Strategies

Do you want to teach someone to spell? Then adjust your expectations to fit that person's needs, abilities, and maturity. All children progress through spelling stages.

What do we expect from a child under age five? This is the *readiness stage* of writing. We'll see scribbling—just to fill up a page. We'll see filling up a page with any letter the child knows. That's spelling. A young child can even read what he wrote back to you! It may be a shopping list, or a Christmas wish list, but he can read it!

Give him the opportunity, and a four to six-year-old will attempt to copy words. He might pick up his favorite book and try to copy from it. Never mind that the letters are sprawled all over the page with no spaces in-between. Copying is the natural next step in the progression of learning to spell.

Young beginning writers start trying some of the phonics they learned when you taught them to read. They spell a word the way it sounds (or the way *they* say it.) Seven-year-old Rachel wrote a note to her mother telling her she wanted to "bi a camr." (Translate that "buy a camera.") Beginning writers know letters represent sounds. They simply try out what you taught them! *Let your young child write freely without demanding perfection* (in your eyes). A child overly concerned about perfection (in spelling, handwriting, *or* English mechanics), refuses to write on his own. *Encourage your young writers!* Gradually they'll use the spelling strategies you teach in your phonics lessons!

(By the way, at this point, don't be surprised if reading "takes off" and spelling lags behind awhile. Children who are building reading fluency can usually read many more words than they can spell.)

As reading fluency builds, a writer in *transition* asks himself, *"Does this word look right? Is the number '2' spelled "tow" or "two"*? He'll attempt different spellings of a word until he thinks he's got it right.

But what about the born perfectionist? You know, the one who can't go on with life unless every word is spelled accurately the first go-round? Remind that child the purpose of writing is to *tell you his ideas*. If he stops each time he doesn't know how to spell a word, he's going to lose his thoughts. Encourage him to "just put something down for now" since all writing is done in steps and this step is the equivalent of a young child's rough draft. Maintaining the flow of meaning is the most important aspect of the writing process in the first draft. Putting your ideas on paper is the goal! If we need to polish this piece, we'll do it another day, after we've gotten all our thoughts on paper. After all, that's the way the professional writers do it!

Your dialogue might go something like this:

> *"Mom, I don't know how to spell this word."*
>
> *"Just spell it the best you can. Don't worry about it for now."*

Meanwhile, make words easily accessible to *young* writers. Provide them with a young child's dictionary (see Appendix D and save *Webster's Unabridged* for later—much later) or a small erasable white board at their desks. If the fact that he does not know an accurate spelling interrupts his "writing flow," or if you find your child resisting certain words because they seem too hard, just quickly and silently write the word on the white board. Or, have him consult his easy dictionary. This is *not* the time for an impromptu phonics lesson. Instead, make a mental note of the lesson you'll teach in the near future.

What will be the result of this free writing? You'll have a child who writes much more—with much less effort. And guess what. More writing will lead to more opportunities to experiment with spelling patterns. And the more your child attempts to spell words in the context of his own writing, the better speller he'll become! (By the way, children who spend most of their time filling the blanks in workbooks, have little time left to figure out spelling in the context of actual writing! *Ease up on the workbooks if you want your child to really learn to spell!*)

By now, we hope we have a somewhat mature speller who sees most of his own spelling errors when he proofreads. (Not necessarily while he's writing for meaning.) He's simply "caught on" to spelling with your brief phonics lessons and his ample writing practice. But something else happened. He built a visual recollection of the way words should look and he had the chance to use that recollection when writing. How did he build a visual recollection? *By reading widely*. The more a child reads, the sharper that visual memory becomes . . . in most cases, that is.

What about the person, child or adult, who simply can't see his own spelling mistakes? Your nine, ten or eleven-year-old spells "birthday," "brthday." Or "with" is spelled "whith." A "lifetime poor speller" doesn't remember how words should look! When he proofreads, he simply doesn't "see" even the most obvious misspellings. We're going to help him solve that problem!

❦ Chapter 3 ❦

How Do We Actually Teach Spelling?

(grades 3 & up)

This spelling notebook doesn't come with a prepackaged word list to study. I left it out because I wanted you to focus on your own child's spelling problems. That's what your child needs and besides, it's more efficient! So where do we begin?

Force your child to USE spelling in the context of his own writing. Children are forced to *think about spelling* when they write. There, I said it again! Write something every day—journals, letters, paragraphs, descriptions, explanations, posters, lists . . . you get the idea. Tell him not to worry about spelling when he's brainstorming or writing his first draft—"going for the flow." Some writing, such as journaling, will start and end with the first draft since not every written piece has to be polished.

Other compositions are more special. Older children (ages 8 and up) should polish one piece of writing each week. Remind them that writing is a process. We brainstorm the first day and write for the flow the second day. Then we revise and edit on the final day. Always let a paper cool a day or two before you check the spelling.

Important: The student ***must edit his own final draft*** before he gives it to you. Remember, we're trying to train our children to see their own mistakes. How will they learn to proofread if we don't give them the opportunity? Don't fall into the trap of being your child's sole proofreader. If you take over this step, you've denied the child the opportunity to think about spelling.

By the way, now is a good time to introduce typing and the word processor to your child—but beware! In order to learn to spell, a child using this spelling approach must promise to categorize the misspellings the spellcheck finds. How else will they find out what spelling patterns they need to learn? I tell my students, "*If your goal is to learn how to spell, then you're going to have to cooperate with me for a little while. You must promise me that you will not push a spellcheck button until you have first proofread for your own mistakes. Then, any errors the spellcheck finds should be categorized in your spelling notebook. You must check your own spelling before you go to the spellcheck!*" Older children using the computer, must promise me that after they use the spellcheck and find more errors, they will categorize those errors the computer found.

(Note: Students working on a computer should print the paper and proofread the hard copy. Don't try to find spelling errors on the computer screen!)

Once the student has polished and written a final draft, it's your turn to have a go at it. Please, when you are marking a student's final draft, *be gentle. Use light pencil marks only.* When a person writes, he's opened himself up to the world. If the cost of making mistakes is too great, the writer will stop taking chances. How many of you remember using an easier word in your papers when you were unsure of a spelling? For a young child, age 8-12, put a light pencil dot over the misspelled word. For a highschooler, put a dot in the margin and say, "*Check this line for an error.*"

We're going to teach our children that our language is really quite predictable. If we understand just a few patterns in our language (see the student's notebook, **Tricks of the Trade**), we can spell with at least 90% accuracy. What a comfort! Most children discover a few key areas of need, remedy those areas, and are well on their way to accurate spelling. For example, twelve-year-old Amy discovered she confused the short 'e' and short 'i' sounds in words of three or more syllables. Eleven-year-old Heather found her greatest problem was remembering to *spell by syllables.* See that word "remember" in the last sentence? Heather used to spell it "rember."

What else can we do to teach our children to spell? What about all those spelling rules? I suggest you ***teach only the most frequently used rules***. Memorizing rarely used rules contributes to the already frustrated child's "*Oh, what's the use?*" attitude. But a few spelling rules really are dependable. When teaching a spelling workshop recently I asked the audience (all home educators) to tell me the most frequently used spelling rules. What a brilliant group! They were able to list all of them sight unseen. Turn to

Appendix A and see if you, too, remember the most frequently used spelling rules . . . Do you know why you remembered them? Because they were useful to you!

Teach a child to spell by syllables. Syllables are our words' building blocks. If we spell each syllable in turn, we usually spell the word correctly. Syllables fall into a few simple categories (see **Tricks of the Trade**). Once the student knows the categories, he can easily spell most syllables and thus most words. Long words like 'manufacture' are really not that difficult when they are broken down into syllables: man/ u/ fac/ ture

Encourage good language habits. When a child speaks, require him to enunciate each syllable carefully. If you omit syllables when you speak, you'll omit syllables when you write. For example, Thomas spelled operator, "oprator." He simply needed to learn the word's correct pronunciation! And, if your child has trouble with baby talk or dropped word endings, realize you'll have to deal with it. Speech affects spelling.

Teach your child to pay attention to details. Pay attention to the syllables in each word and the sounds in each syllable. One half of the students in my high school class who started this spelling program experienced overnight success. I'm convinced they found it was easier to pay attention to details when proofreading than it was to categorize misspelled words in their individualized notebooks!

And speaking of carelessness, if your child is a careless reader (in the name of reading 'fast') **teach him to**

periodically slow down and read closely for details. Speed readers can be prone to overlooking spelling details (not to mention subtle meanings in what they read.) There is a time to scan quickly for information and a time for careful, reflective reading. Have your child do both. Read extensively. Reflect. Ponder. And observe details.

❦ Chapter 4 ❦

The Building Blocks

Consonants, Vowels, Syllables

Each child's spelling needs are specific. If he's a fluent reader, he's already absorbed a lot of spelling patterns. Now your job as a tutor is to help him discover exactly what else he needs to learn.

Poor spellers are usually greatly relieved to find written language is predictable. Even if they were taught to read with phonics, they might not realize spelling has patterns, too. Explaining written language patterns solves much of the problem.

It's really not that complicated. Just tell your students words are made from building blocks. If we know a little about the blocks that build words, we can spell just about anything. The first building blocks are called consonants. **Consonants** are sounds produced by partially obstructed air blocked by the lips, teeth, or tongue. For example, we use our lips to form the sound of **/p/**. Our teeth and tongue make the sound of **/t/**. Make sure your student can clearly enunciate each consonant sound.

The second building blocks are called vowels. **Vowels** are sounds which flow freely from the mouth and throat. The shape of the mouth determines the correct pronunciation of vowels. Say them attached to a simple word (instead of isolated) for practice. Many parents tell me they can't pronounce the vowel sounds. Can you say the following words? (I'll bet you can!) Then, you can enunciate the short vowels!

/a/	a—apple
/e/	e—egg
/i/	i—Indian
/o/	o—olive
/u/	u—up

Use the correct mouth formation for each vowel sound. If your student is having trouble, he should look at your mouth and then into a mirror to see his own mouth. Short **'e'** and short **'i'** are the two easiest vowels to confuse. Again, say them at the beginning of egg and Indian, and they won't be so easily confused.

Consonants and vowels build **syllables.** *Each syllable must have a vowel sound.* (Just knowing that truth solves much of the spelling mystery for some children!) The vowel sound creates the syllable! The count of vowel sounds corresponds to the number of beats (syllables) in a word. For example, 'remedy' has three vowel sounds, three syllables, three beats.

Let's look at the types of syllables you'll encounter in reading and spelling:

C-V-C („hot")

Syllables with a short vowel are called 'closed syllables' because they end with a consonant. (We have to close the air flow from our mouth to say the consonant.) The pattern is 'consonant-vowel-consonant' or C-V-C. The word

'cap' is a closed syllable. Both syllables in **'hab/it'** are closed.

V-C-V
("came")

Syllables with a vowel-consonant-vowel pattern have a long vowel sound. For example, **'tote'** has a V-C-V pattern. So does **'ride'**. What letter keeps the **'i'** in ride long when we add the suffix **'ing'**? **'Riding'**. Now you know why we can drop the **'e'** before adding **'ing.'**

C-V
("we, sta/ble")

Open syllables in words like **'no'** and **'bri/dle'** have a consonant-vowel pattern (C-V). Since the vowel has no consonant after it (in the syllable), it is free to say its own name. If the syllable ended with a consonant, we'd have to close part of our mouth to say it and we can only say long vowels with our mouths *open.* If you don't believe me, try saying each long vowel in front of a mirror.

r-control
(sir, for)

Syllables like **'bird'** in **'birdhouse'** or **'sar'** in **'sarcastic'** are **'r-controlled'** syllables. The letter **'r'** affects the sound of the vowel.

C -le
(tram/ple)

Syllables with **'le'** grab a consonant. For example, we spell **'bub/ble'** with two b's. Since the **'le'** always grabs the consonant in front of it, do you see what would happen to the first syllable in **'bubble'** if we didn't write it with two b's? How do you pronounce **'bu/ble'**? The first syllable needs to end with a consonant in order to keep the letter **'u'** short.

two vowels one unique sound Some syllables have two vowels stuck together to make one unique sound. For example, **'oi'** in **toil** spells **/oy/**. **'Ow'** in **cow** says **/ow/**. Other syllables have two vowels stuck together that say their own name (the long vowel). For example, **'oa'** in oat says **/o/**. The rest of the vowel combinations might not play by the most common rules but they're also used less often. When your child misses an unusual vowel combination, such as **'ou'** says **/oo/** as in **soup**, look up the reason in a resource like *The ABC's and All Their Tricks*. (See Appendix D.) Once he knows the reason, he's likely to recall it when he starts combining *thinking* and proofreading. *(By the way, **'ou'** says **/oo/** in French—most of the words spelled that way are borrowed from the French language. I looked it up.* ☺)

For a more comprehensive look at syllable patterns, see Appendix B: Syllable Patterns: Lessons for Review.

To summarize, tutorial teaching requires no programmed texts, provides no pat answers. You simply find out what spelling patterns are causing a problem today and help your child categorize those patterns. The structure of the language itself forms your scope and sequence chart! And your lessons reflect your student's own needs. Why waste time teaching spelling any other way?

❦ Chapter 5 ❦

The Daily Spelling Lesson

A Perfect Fit

FOR PRIMARY GRADES:

Spelling instruction cannot be separated from actual writing. When our family studied conifers we collected pine cones outside. We experimented a bit with the pine cones. After our experience, the children (ages 8, 6, and 5) retold the event. As they spoke to me I wrote their actual words on a white board so they could all see it. I wrote. They copied. That was a spelling (and writing) lesson for the primary grades.

> "Today we collected pine cones. When Mom baked them in the oven, they blew up. Seeds came out. Mom says that's what happens in a forest fire."

Suppose young children write about an experience for themselves? You see the product and think, "*Oh, great! I'm supposed to send this to Grandmother? I can hardly read it!*" Save some samples of your children's writing just as they're written. Hand copy or retype other passages, especially if they're going to be "made public"! Correct spelling as you go. Store those writing samples and polished drafts in your child's portfolio. He'll not only enjoy reading and re-reading them, he'll have a record of his progress as well. Even young children learn the writing process: we brainstorm, write a rough draft, and polish a final copy for special papers. But YOU bear the burden for the final draft in the primary years. *And* you'll teach spelling in the process! Balance your writing lessons with a *short* daily phonics lesson and *ample* wide reading.

FOR GRADES 3 AND UP:

The Spelling Lesson—Four Simple Steps

Step 1	5 minutes daily phonic review—teach word families, introduce words of several syllables that have the patterns you're learning.
Step 2	5 minutes daily review of words from the child's own spelling notebook. Emphasize *reasoning*, not rote memorization. Gradually add sentence dictation as time allows.
Step 3	10 minutes oral reading with "penciling" to draw the eye of the reader to patterns of words and phrases, as well as enhance visual perception.
Step 4	Write each day.

1. Phonic Review

By the time your child is eight or nine years old, your spelling lesson strategy changes somewhat. Spend 5-10 minutes per day on a simple phonics review. Teach one pattern/word list from the child's individualized spelling notebook or Appendix B of this manual. *"Lets talk about how we spell /oo/ as in zoo. Let's practice this word family."* Practice words of more than one syllable, too: poodle, baboon. Then dictate lists that combine more than one pattern: car/toon, crow/bar. A daily dose of 'phonic vitamins' will remind the child of the patterns found in our language. Avoid presenting potentially confusing information on the same day. Just as we wouldn't present the short **'e'** and the short **'i'** in the same reading lesson for a young beginner, we wouldn't teach both <u>sounds</u> of **'ei'** (**receive, neighbor**) at the same spelling lesson.

2. Categorize, Review & Reason

Actual writing must be a regular component of written language instruction. Without it, all the spelling drill in the world won't "stick"! Give your child ample opportunity to practice (through application) new learning until it becomes automatic. Have him write something new each week and proofread his own paper. When he's done his best, he should bring the paper to you and the two of you should examine the paper together for errors. Correct misspelled words and categorize them (together, at first) in the child's individualized spelling notebook. Discuss the reason the word was misspelled and develop a strategy for remembering it the next time.

So, the child has written amply, proofread his papers, and categorized his own spelling errors in his individualized spelling notebook. There's one more step to take in order to insure success! Spend five minutes *each* day, reviewing the words the child has accumulated in his *own* spelling notebook. Dictate the words. Have the student repeat each syllable, pronounce its vowel sound, and spell each syllable aloud. Then have the student write each syllable, naming each letter as he writes it. After writing the word, the student reads each syllable he has written, *pencil in hand**. (I'll tell you in a minute why the pencil should be in his hand.)

Be sure to associate the syllables of the written word with the patterns listed in the child's notebook. For example, do you see why **happen** has **two p's**? It's because **hap** is a closed syllable (C-V-C) and it needs a **'p'** following that **'a'** to keep it short. Or, do you see why **puzzle** has **two z's**? The **'le'** grabs the consonant in front of it and we need to close off that first syllable with a consonant in order to keep the **'u'** short. Constant reinforcement of newly learned associations is the key to success here. (See student's book: ***Tricks of the Trade,*** and Appendix B for patterns to teach.)

(**Note:** Don't make this simply an oral drill—spelling is *written* language.)

For clarity, here's a breakdown of Step 2: Categorize, Review & Reason

1. Dictate word(s) from the child's individualized spelling notebook.

2. Student repeats word and says its vowel sound.

3. Student writes word as he says each syllable and, in turn, each letter as he writes it.

4. Student "pencils" each syllable of the word after it is written.

5. Teacher reminds student of the "building block pattern" the word follows.

(**Note:** This spelling lesson does not consist of copying a list of words or spelling orally. And remember, it's important to pronounce the word syllable-by-syllable and write each syllable as it is pronounced.)

3. 'Penciling'

I suggest that you teach syllable structure to your children with a technique I call 'penciling'. When teaching a word, simply draw "swoops" under each syllable like this: fan tas tic. When you dictate individualized spelling word lists to your child, always have him "pencil" the syllables of the word after he writes it. Penciling (a kinesthetic movement) forces the eye to focus and reinforces what we're after— *paying attention to spelling patterns.*

By the way, penciling can also be used for reading passages. As the child reads you follow the line of print with a pencil. If he stumbles on a word, don't say it, "swoop" the pencil under each syllable. Let the child recall the associations he's learned on his own. Penciling has the added benefit of forcing the student to focus on <u>sequencing</u> of syllables and sounds.

4. Write Each Day

Heard this advice before?

Gradually, your student should assume responsibility for his own learning. As he becomes capable of independent work and self assessment, he should categorize and review his own spelling errors. Before you know it, he'll conquer his own spelling problems. As Mark Twain said, "Use a new word correctly three times and it's yours for life." I believe this is as true for spelling (in the context of writing, of course) as it is for vocabulary!

Now that we've discussed how children really learn to spell, you're well on your way to teaching spelling effectively way. Before you start, take a glance at the Appendix A: Rules Worth Remembering, just to reassure yourself that this can't be that hard, after all. Then, check your spelling tutor's toolbox to see that you have everything you need. You're well on your way to meeting your own students' individualized spelling needs! Happy tutoring!

Gayle Graham

Tutor's Toolbox

- one individualized spelling notebook ***per child***
  (Tricks of the Trade)
- writing samples
- pencil, paper
- a good dictionary
- a good phonic encyclopedia for the teacher

❦ Appendix A ❦

Rules Worth Remembering

Rule 1

Change the "Y" to "I" and add the suffix.

Examples: happy – happiness
fly – flies

Note! Don't change the "Y" if it means you'll have 3 vowels in a row.

Examples: lay – lays, (not laies)
monkey – monkeys,
(not monkeies)

Rule 2

"I" before "E" except after "C" and when it says "A" as in neighbor and weigh.

Examples: yield
receive

Rule 3

Drop the silent "e" before adding a suffix that begins with a vowel.

Examples: come – coming
safe – safer
move – movable

Note! Change one "I" to "Y" to prevent 2 "I's" from coming together.

Example: tie – tying (not tiing)

Note! If the word ends in "CE" or "GE" and the suffix begins with "A" or "O," keep the "E." (How would you say chan<u>ga</u>ble?)

Example: change – changeable

Note! Keep the "e" on verbs ending in "oe" to preserve the pronunciation.

Examples: canoe – canoeing
hoe – hoeing

Rule 4

Change the "f" to "v" and add "es."

Example: calf – calves

Rule 5

Use "k" before "e" or "i" to make the /k/ sound.

Examples: kitten
picnic – picnicking

Note! If you used 'c' alone (picnicing), it would say /s/.

Use 'C' before the other vowels to produce the /k/ sound.

Example: cupboard

Rule 6

If you have a *one syllable word* that ends with a single consonant, double that consonant before adding a suffix that begins with a vowel.

Example: run – running

Note! If we didn't double the consonant, the word would be ru/ning, with a long U sound.

Note! If you have a two syllable word that ends with a single consonant, double the consonant before adding the suffix that begins with a vowel <u>only</u> if the second syllable is accented. (I know it's a mouthful but it's a mouthful worth remembering! Read it again slowly and study the examples.)

Examples: ad mit' – admitting
trav' el – traveled

Rule 6 (again!)

Another way of saying the above is, double the consonant if you need to.

Example: kennel, *not* kenel
pro/pel/ler, *not* pro/pe/ler

Why? Divide the word into syllables and you'll see ken/nel says what we want it to say. 'Ke/nel' leaves the first syllable open, producing a long e sound.

❦ Appendix B ❦

The Daily Phonic Review

One important facet of remediating spelling is the daily phonic review. I tell my students to consider the phonic review something like a daily dose of medicine. It might not "taste" great, but it's part of the prescription for the problem at hand: solving all your spelling woes!

Just as you'd never even consider administering an entire bottle of penicillin all at once to your child, you won't try to review all the spelling patterns in a day! (Or in a month, for that matter!) Frequent small doses (10 minutes/day, 3 times/week) will do the trick!

For your lesson, teach one phonic rule and a few words that use the spelling pattern. (I've listed a few words to get you started.) Proceed through the rules and lists in the order provided. Don't go on to the next rule until the former is mastered. In other words, over-teach the rules until they become automatic. Review previously learned rules and sample words frequently.

If you find you need more word examples than I've offered, consult a dictionary. Or, put your student to work finding examples in magazines, newspapers, or his own reading material.

When you teach the spelling patterns, use a large white board or chalkboard instead of a sheet of paper and pencil. It's more effective! After teaching, dictate the words to your student. For variety, allow your student to write the dictated words on the board.

Since children learn best when they use all their senses, be sure your child vocalizes the syllables as he writes them (auditory). Encourage him to use his whole arm when he writes on the board (kinesthetic). Then, tell him to step back and look at what he's written. Does the word "look" right? (visual)

Some rules in your student's individualized spelling notebook won't have practice word lists in this appendix. That's simply because those rules aren't used frequently enough to warrant a list. Avoid phonic overkill. Instead, teach spelling patterns only as the need occurs in your student's own writing. Then, together with your child, find and practice other words which use the same pattern.

Remember, reviewing phonics is only a tiny part of the whole spelling picture! Just as you'd never feed a child only vitamins, you'd not consider teaching only phonic rules without daily free writing: journals, lists, notes, prayers, instructions, and the like. That's real food for spelling growth!

Rules and Lists

CONSONANTS

c says /k/

cat cut cob
camp cute cost
came cub cover

c says /s/

cell city bicycle
fence pencil fancy
face cider cyst

g says /g/

gale got gut
gal goal gulf
game good gull

g says /j/

ginger age giant
gist gelatin origin
gentle stage

ch says /ch/

chin chop child
peach chip chat

ch says /k/

chemistry mechanic character

ch says /sh/

machine Michelle parachute

ng says /ng/

hang spring long
sang lung strong

nk says /nk/

sink bunk drink
thank honk blank

ph says /f/

photo dolphin alphabet

sh says /sh/

slash cast trash

wh says /wh/

wheel which where
whale when wharf

th

that those either
there these weather

th

think tooth method
thick thing ethnic

k says /k/

kite brook kitchen

qu says /kw/

queen quite queer
in qui si tive

SHORT VOWELS

a			e		
catnap	shag	fast	stem	den	expect
add	grasp	sand	tent	emblem	helmet
			pretzel		
i			**o**		
tip	skim	crisp	prod	top	frost
tidbit	windmill	distill	not	loft	bon bon
u			**y**		
drum	hut	fund	hymn	Flynn	Lynn
fungus	crust	grunt			

LONG VOWELS - SILENT E

a			e		
came	grade	bade	mere	here	complete
spade			theme		
i			**o**		
die	pie	chime	vote	hope	alone
divide			antelope		
u			**y**		
luke	fumes	rule	rhyme	typewriter	dye
use			rye		

OPEN VOWEL SYLLABLES

a	e
potato cable baby	she even belief rebate
i	**o**
spider pilot cider	robot hero produce
u	**y**
music visual human	reply lying myself

R-CONTROLLED SYLLABLES

ar	er	ir
marry sparrow barrel carry	very perish heron America	bird confirm birthday
ur	**or**	**or**
surface urban frankfurter	world worm worship	pork color record
yr		
syrup lyric		

CONSONANT -LE SYLLABLES

	le	
needle	maple	candle
apple	title	pestle
giggle		

❦ Appendix C ❦

Frequently Misspelled Words

A few words are downright pesky. Wait! Review this list *after* your student masters (in the context of his own writing) the most frequently used spelling patterns.

always

beginning
believe
built
business
buy

color

doctor
does

every

February
forty
friend

grammar
guess

half

instead
just

lose

meant

often
once

piece

raise
read
ready

said
says
separate
since
sugar

their
there
they're
though
through
two

Wednesday
where
whether
which
women

❦ Appendix D ❦

Recommended Materials for Teaching Spelling

Provide your young writer with the opportunity to take responsibility for his own spelling:

Words I Use When I Write
by Alana Trisler and Patrice Howe Cardiel

An easy-to-use spelling dictionary for the beginning writer, grades 1-2. Words are listed in large handwritten print and space is provided for you to write extra words when they are requested. Even includes contractions.

A Spelling Dictionary for Beginning Writers
by Gregory Hurray

Contains 1400 of the words most frequently used by early elementary writers, including inflected forms placed next to their root words (come/coming.) Word bank in the back provides mini-thesaurus. Print is type-style and large enough for "seven-year-old eyes." Approximate grade level: (2-5.)

The ABC's and All Their Tricks
by Margaret M. Bishop

A *complete* encyclopedia of spellings for every sound. Any spelling question that arises can be easily answered with this quick reference book.

Letters and letter combinations are listed alphabetically. For each spelling, you find rules which control it, exceptions, and word lists for practice. The reason I like this book so much is because I can find exactly what I need to know in it so quickly!

A Measuring Scale For Ability in Spelling
by Leonard Porter Ayers

A scale for measuring your children's ability in spelling. Lists 1000 most commonly used words among school children. All children should learn to spell these 1000 words since they use them so often.

Natural Speller
by Kathryn Stout

The practice one child needs could be just 'busy work' for another. This book provides you with the means to design spelling lessons that include dictionary use, vocabulary, phonics, punctuation, writing, grammar, and homonyms. You decide what to include in each lesson based on your own children's needs.

How to Teach Any Child to Spell
by Gayle Graham

Frustrated with memorized but forgotten workbooks? Wondering how you'll ever get to the heart of your student's spelling problems? In this little book, Gayle Graham offers a common-sense solution for all your student's spelling woes. Use with student's spelling notebook, *Tricks of the Trade*.

Tricks of the Trade
by Gayle Graham

The student's own individualized spelling notebook helps him classify his own errors and thus pinpoint his own spelling needs. This tool gets to the heart of the child's <u>own</u> spelling problems. Accompanies *How to Teach Any Child to Spell* by Gayle Graham.

Type It
by Joan Duffy

Reinforces spelling patterns while teaching touch typing. I teach my children typing with this manual on the computer keyboard. So easy! Use for children ages 8 and up.